WHERE PEOPLE LIVE

Living in Cities

Neil Morris

FRANKLIN WATTS
LONDON•SYDNEY

 An Appleseed Editions book

First published in 2004 by Franklin Watts
96 Leonard Street, London, EC2A 4XD

Franklin Watts Australia
45–51 Huntley Street, Alexandria, NSW 2015

© 2004 Appleseed Editions

Created by Appleseed Editions Ltd,
Well House, Friars Hill, Guestling, East Sussex, TN35 4ET

Designed by Helen James

ISBN 0 7496 5833 9

A CIP catalogue for this book is available from the British Library.

Photographs by Corbis (AFP, CAMPBELL WILLIAM/CORBIS SYGMA, Stephanie Colasanti, Dean Conger, Sergio Dorantes, Macduff Everton, Marc Garanger, Colin Garratt; Milepost 92 1/2, Martyn Goddard, Gunter Marx Photography, Robert Holmes, Dave G. Houser, Wolfgang Kaehler, Richard Klune, Brooks Kraft, Bob Krist, Danny Lehman, Charles & Josette Lenars, Pawel Libera, Chris Lisle, Wally McNamee, Carl & Ann Purcell, Vittoriano Rastelli, Carmen Redondo, Reuters, Hugh Rooney; Eye Ubiquitous, Bill Ross, Alan Schein Photography, Uwe Schmid, Joseph Sohm; ChromoSohm Inc., Paul A. Souders, Steve Starr, Ken Straiton, Nik Wheeler, Adam Woolfitt)

Printed in the USA

Contents

Introduction

There have been cities for thousands of years. Today, the world's biggest cities have millions of people living and working in them. Most cities are growing bigger all the time as people move there from the countryside. In 1950, less than one-third of the world's people lived in towns and cities. By the end of the century, this figure had grown to nearly half. Experts think that by 2025 at least two-thirds of the population will live in **urban** areas. More and more of the world's people are getting to know what it's like to live in a city.

 *This **monorail** takes people around Sydney, the biggest city in Australia, quickly and in comfort.*

Spreading out

Cities grow outwards from their centre, where there are usually tall buildings, shops, and offices. Few people live right in the city centre, because there is so little space and the cost of housing is too high. There are more houses and apartment buildings in the outer city, and even more further out in the **suburbs**. Most city-dwellers, therefore, actually live many miles away from their city centre, and many of them travel in to work every day.

The Old Town of Stockholm, capital of Sweden. In the last 50 years, Stockholm has grown and taken in other towns as suburbs. Whole sections of the city have been rebuilt to make new housing for its growing population.

Friends and neighbours

In cities, there are many different local neighbourhoods. These are located right next to each other, and this is what makes cities such interesting places. Sometimes people from similar backgrounds or with similar interests stick together and form their own **community**. Many large cities have their own Chinatown, for example, where Chinese people live and work. Sometimes there are disagreements and tensions between different communities, but most people get along with their friends and neighbours.

Many thousands of Chinese people live in the Chinatown district of Vancouver, Canada. The district's main street is full of restaurants and shops.

5

The world's first cities were built in a region that historians call Mesopotamia, in modern Iraq and Syria. Ancient people called Sumerians founded one of the earliest cities about 3500 BC. The city, called Ur, was built beside the Euphrates River and became an important **port**. Like many early cities, it was a sacred centre, where kings and priests could worship their gods. At Ur, the Sumerians built a pyramid-shaped, stepped tower called a ziggurat for their most important god, the moon god, Nanna. The ziggurat stood in the walled inner city. As more people came to Ur, they made an outer city that was probably five times bigger than the inner area.

 All we can see at Ur today is the restored first level of the ziggurat. It originally had two more levels, with a shrine to the moon god on top.

The birthplace of Western civilization

Athens, the capital of modern Greece, began as a small **settlement** around 3000 BC. It became an important city 1,800 years later. Like Ur, it had its own king and became a **city-state**, ruling over the surrounding countryside. The Athenians built a fortified district for their main religious buildings,

called the Acropolis (meaning 'city at the top"), on a hill overlooking the city. At the city centre was a wide, open space called an agora, which served as a market place and meeting area. From 682 BC, elected officials governed Athens, which became the artistic centre of ancient Greece. Because of this, it is often called the birthplace of Western civilization. Unlike Ur, the city survives to this day, with a 21st century population of about three million.

▲ *The main building on the Acropolis of Athens is called the Parthenon. This famous temple of the goddess Athena dates from 438 BC.*

The Eternal City

According to legend, Rome was founded in 753 BC by Romulus, who, with his twin brother, Remus, was found abandoned on the banks of the Tiber River. The babies were looked after by a she-wolf and founded a city on the Palatine Hill, which is still in central Rome today. This was one of seven hills that provided the setting for the city that grew to become the capital of the great Roman Empire. Rome is still the capital of modern Italy today, and it is called the 'Eternal City' because it has survived for so long.

◄ *The Colosseum was completed in AD 80. It was built so that 50,000 Romans could watch gladiator contests and even mock sea battles.*

Rebuilding the Past

Throughout history, cities have been destroyed – mainly by war – and then rebuilt. One of the best examples is the old capital of the Aztec empire, in Mexico. According to legend, the wandering Aztec people were told by a god to look for a special sign – an eagle perched on a cactus grasping a snake – and settle where they found it. Around 1325, the Aztecs found the sign they were looking for, on a marshy island in a lake. They settled there, drained the land to make a village, and then built **causeways** to the mainland. By 1400, the village, called Tenochtitlan, had grown into a large, important city with up to 300,000 **inhabitants**. In 1519, however, Spanish conquerors arrived, and within two years, they had destroyed the Aztec capital. But another, new capital was to rise from the ruins – Mexico City.

Mexico City

The Spanish conquerors built a new city on top of the ruins of Tenochtitlan and made Mexico City the capital of their **colony** of New Spain. Since that time, natural disasters have forced inhabitants to rebuild the city twice. After 30,000 people died in floods in 1629, the lake was drained, and the canal system was improved. By the late 20th century, the city, which had become the capital of independent Mexico, was one of

 At the centre of Tenochtitlan was a Great Temple. The Spaniards destroyed this, but Mexican builders rediscovered its ruins in 1978.

Mexico City lies 2,240 metres above sea level and is surrounded by mountains. ▶

the biggest in the world. Then, in 1985, it was hit by an earthquake. More than 400 buildings collapsed, another 3,000 were badly damaged, and about 10,000 people were killed.

German capital

Berlin was founded as a trading village in the early 13th century. Over hundreds of years it grew into a town and then a city, and became the capital of Germany in 1871. During World War II (1939–1945), Berlin was flattened by bombs. After the war, it was divided between the two countries of West and East Germany, and a wall was put up to stop people from moving from one half to the other. In 1989, the Berlin Wall was knocked down, the two countries reunified (joined together again), and the following year Berlin once again became the capital of one, united Germany. Since then, there has been a huge building programme to turn the capital into an exciting city for modern Berliners.

▼ *Berlin's Brandenburg Gate is seen as a symbol of reunified Germany. It was built in 1791 in the style of the original gateway to the Acropolis in Athens (see page 7).*

Trade and Industry

Most cities grew up because they were important trading places. The ancient Chinese city of Chang'an, for example, lay at the eastern end of the Silk Road, a trade route that was more than 6,000 kilometres long. At that time, China maintained a profitable silk trade with western Asia and Europe. Chang'an became the capital of the Chinese Empire during the Tang dynasty (AD 618–907), and in the eighth century it was probably the largest city in the world. It was a planned city, with a grid-shaped network of streets around an imperial park and two large markets. The basic layout of Chang'an was later followed at Beijing, when it became the imperial capital hundreds of years later.

▲ *Modern Xi'an (built on ancient Chang'an) has a population of more than 2.8 million. Its factories produce chemicals, electronic equipment, paper and textiles.*

Industrial port

During the **Industrial Revolution**, Liverpool, in north-west England, became one of the world's greatest ports. The first dock was built there in 1715, and by the end of the 18th century, the growing city had more docks than London. During the 1800s, Liverpool became the major port for Europeans sailing to the United

The Albert Dock, in Liverpool, was opened in 1846. It no longer deals with ships but today has an art gallery, a maritime museum, shops and restaurants. The dock attracts six million visitors a year. ▶

States. But by the middle of the 20th century, the city's industries were in decline: passengers were crossing the Atlantic by air instead of by sea, and the docks were scarcely being used for **cargo** such as wool and cotton. This meant that many Liverpudlians had difficulty finding work.

Place of gold

Cities grow quickly when their location has something special to offer people. In 1886, gold was found in the region of present-day Johannesburg, in South Africa. A town was founded there, and gold prospectors flocked from all over the world. Many came and went, but by 1896, the growing city was home to more than 100,000 people. It became the centre of South Africa's gold-mining industry and was made capital of the new province of Gauteng in 1994. Today, more than three million people live in Johannesburg, the city that South Africans call the 'place of gold'.

◀ *More than 40 percent of the world's gold has come from the bustling city of Johannesburg, South Africa.*

Megacities

When huge cities keep on growing, they sometimes join up with nearby towns and cities. We call the world's biggest settlements 'megacities'. The biggest of them all is Tokyo, the capital of Japan, which is home to 28 million people. That's almost three times as many people as in Paris, and nearly four times as many as in London. In fact, as many people live in the central city area of Tokyo as live in each of those two European cities combined. This naturally means that everything is very crowded in Tokyo, which is full of high-rise (multistorey) offices and shops, as well as apartment blocks and other homes. This amazing megacity was twice rebuilt in the last century. In 1923, it was almost completely destroyed by a violent earthquake. Then, in 1945, the city was again left in ruins after being severely bombed during World War II. The population was then just 3.5 million, which shows how much this megacity has grown over the past 60 years.

Trying to stop growth

In South America, the government of Brazil has tried in recent years to stop the city of São Paulo from growing any further. The city has more than 17 million inhabitants, and people have been encouraged to move to different areas of Brazil. This plan has not been very successful, however. São Paulo was founded by Christian missionaries (who named the settlement after St. Paul) in 1554. Centuries later, the growing town became the centre of

The high-rise shopping district of Ginza, Tokyo, lights up the night.

Brazil's coffee industry, and in the late 19th century, the population suddenly grew from 30,000 to 240,000. Today, the city's main industries include the production of textiles, electrical goods, and furniture. Unfortunately, millions of Paulistanos (the people of São Paulo) have no job or earn very little. Many live in sprawling **shanty** suburbs.

Chinese City

Shanghai is the most **populous** city in the world's most populous country – China. But whereas 1 in every 5 Japanese lives in Tokyo, just 1 in every 90 Chinese lives in Shanghai. This huge megacity began as a small trading port about 800 years ago. Its oldest district, which is often called Chinese City, has narrow streets that are usually crowded with **pedestrians** and cyclists. Nearby is the Pudong district, which was built in the 1990s. This new zone has industrial parks, factories and high-rise housing estates. Many factory workers and their families have moved to this district.

13

Lifestyles

People have developed their own special ways of living in the city. The most obvious difference between urban and **rural** lifestyles is in housing. In the city, people live and work close together, and city buildings have grown upwards to gain space. The first **skyscrapers** appeared in the United States, in Chicago. In 1871, a fire destroyed much of the city, and **architects** began redesigning it. The 10 floors of the first high-rise building went up in 1885, and it was soon followed by much larger structures. Chicago's tallest skyscraper is the 110-storey, 443-metre tall Sears Tower, which is an enormous office block. Skyscrapers are used for people's homes, too. The 100-storey John Hancock Center contains more than 700 apartments, as well as offices. Many cities around the world have developed in a similar way.

Artistic architecture

For many centuries, architects have tried to design city buildings that are good to live in and good to look at. Some cities have become famous for a special kind of architecture. The Spanish city of Barcelona, for example, is famous for the unique buildings created by Antoni Gaudí (1852–1926). He designed one of his greatest buildings, Casa

 In Chicago, many people have a wonderful view of Lake Michigan from their apartment window.

Gaudí's Casa Milà stands on a busy street corner in Barcelona. People who did not like its new and very different design called the building La Pedrera ('the stone quarry').

Milà, as an apartment block. When the eight-storey building was finished, in 1910, it even had an underground car park. At the time, people thought the building looked strange, and it was not popular. Today, people come from all over the world to admire it.

Family homes

Modern cities, such as Chicago, have grown upwards, but many older cities were already full of houses, and it has been more difficult for them to find additional space. London, which was founded by the Romans almost 2,000 years ago, has many streets full of **terraced** and **semi-detached houses**. Many were built in the 19th and 20th centuries as family houses, though some of the larger versions have since been split up into flats. After World War II, some housing estates full of high-rise blocks of flats were built. These were so unpopular with Londoners that many have since been torn down.

These terraced houses in London enable a large number of people to live in a relatively small area.

Capital Cities

Every country in the world has a capital, which is its city of government. This is where the country's laws are made and its most important decisions are debated. The capital is often a country's biggest city, but not always. Washington, DC, the capital of the United States, is the sixth biggest U.S. city (New York, Los Angeles, Chicago, Philadelphia, and San Francisco all have more people). It was chosen as the capital in 1791 by President George Washington, who hired a French architect to plan out the city on land that belonged to the federal government (called the District of Columbia, or DC). The U.S. government moved in 1800 from its temporary home in Philadelphia to Washington, which then had about 8,000 inhabitants. Today, this number has grown to almost four million, and many Washingtonians are still employed by the government.

The White House, at 1600 Pennsylvania Avenue in Washington, DC, is the official residence of the President of the United States. More than one million people visit it each year.

Old and New Delhi

In 1912, the capital of India was moved from Calcutta to Delhi, an old city that had been founded in the 12th century. However, the British governors of India decided that the country needed a new, specially planned capital. They built the new capital just to the south of the old city and called it New Delhi. This city, which has broad streets spreading out from its centre like the spokes of a wheel, took over as capital in 1931. It has a population of just 300,000, compared with old Delhi's seven million. Many of

A military parade in honour of Republic Day, an Indian national holiday, passes along a tree-lined avenue in New Delhi.

the new city's people work for the Indian government, and they live in modern buildings on **boulevards**. In the old city, most people live in small houses on crowded, narrow streets.

City on the Nile

Cairo, the capital of Egypt, was founded in 969 by Fatimid Arabs. They built a small walled city and called it al-Qahirah (meaning 'the victorious'), which in English became 'Cairo'. The following year, the Fatimids founded a university, and Cairo has remained a city of learning ever since. Over more than a thousand years, the city has grown in an unplanned way. Unlike Washington, DC, and New Delhi, it has many narrow, crowded streets. Wealthy Cairenes (the people of Cairo), many of whom work for the government, live in new suburbs outside the city.

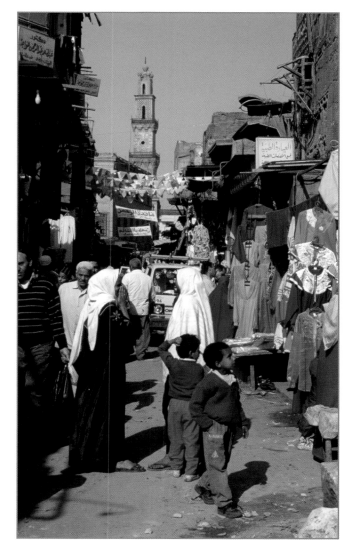

Poorer people work in Cairo factories and small shops, and they live in small apartments and houses in the old districts.

Cities within Cities

Many of the world's cities are overcrowded. Urban areas continue to attract people from the countryside, who are often unskilled or have had little education and find it difficult to get work. This has led to **poverty** and overcrowding in the big cities of developing countries all over the world. Unemployed (jobless) people or those with low incomes crowd together in poor districts, where they make their own houses. These are often little more than shacks made of wood, metal or even cardboard. The makeshift homes are usually without running water, proper lavatories, or drains, yet often all the members of a large family have to live together in one flimsy shack.

In many of the world's large cities, the distance between wealth and poverty is not very great.

Brazilian *favelas*

In some large Brazilian cities, such as Rio de Janeiro, up to one-fifth of the population may live in **slum** districts, called *favelas* in Portuguese. There are hundreds of *favelas* in Rio and many in São Paulo (see page 12). Many of the Rio settlements are on hillsides overlooking the city. Heavy rain often causes dangerous mudslides that simply wash the shacks away. The poverty and poor conditions also mean that

Self-built shanties line the hillsides surrounding Rio de Janeiro, Brazil.

favela-dwellers suffer from **malnutrition** and diseases that could easily be cured with the right medicines. The Brazilian government has replaced some shanty towns with better, low-cost housing, but there is still great poverty.

Indonesian problems

Jakarta, on the south-east Asian island of Java, is the capital of Indonesia. Since the country gained independence in 1949, Jakarta has grown enormously, with many people moving from the countryside to try and find work. Traditionally, Javanese people live in small wooden houses in districts called *kampongs*. In Jakarta, the great increase in population led to many new slum districts. Because of this, the city's governor banned people from moving to the city unless they had jobs to go to. When the numbers still kept growing, the Indonesian government offered Javanese people free land on the island of Sumatra, where they could have their own small farms. But Jakarta keeps on growing, and its problems continue.

Explosive population growth over the past 50 years has forced many Javanese people into slums.

Getting Around

People use cars, buses, trains, and many other forms of transport to get around in today's big cities. With thousands or even millions of people all travelling at once, a city's transport system needs to be integrated. This means that all the different forms of transport must link up and work well together. This is particularly important during rush hour, when people are travelling to and from work. Private cars are the main cause of traffic jams in cities, and their **exhaust fumes** pollute the air. So it is important to city-dwellers that trains and buses run on time. In many of today's cities, a person can buy one ticket to cover all of a city's different forms of transport, changing from one to the other to get where he or she wants to go easily and quickly.

Underground travel

Londoners were the first to experience an underground railway, or 'tube' as they call it. The London Underground opened in 1863, using steam locomotives. It was an immediate success, and more than nine million passengers were carried in its first year. Today, underground railways in the world's great cities are much more crowded: nearly 10 million people use

▲ *In Lisbon, the capital of Portugal, old cable railways are still used to carry passengers up steep hills.*

Tokyo's **commuter** underground and overland trains every day. During rush hours, special railway workers help push people on to the crowded trains. The people of Moscow are particularly proud of their beautifully designed underground system. Moscow Metro stations are decorated with marble, stained glass, and chandeliers.

Integrated transport

Munich, the largest city in southern Germany, is a good example of integrated transport. A new airport opened 27 kilometres north-east of the city in 1992, and it is connected to the city centre by a fast railway (called the S-Bahn). In the city itself there is an underground railway (U-Bahn), which connects with the overland railway as well as with modern trams and buses on the streets. One ticket covers all of these. Cyclists are also very welcome in Munich. On most streets there are special cycleways, so many people use their bike to get around.

Cycling is a fast, efficient way to travel the streets of Munich, Germany.

21

Shopping

Small shops and large stores form an important feature of any city. People expect to be able to buy whatever they want in a city's shopping district. This is a useful service for city-dwellers, and the shops also provide them with jobs. Some of the world's biggest cities have become famous for certain goods. For example, London, Milan, New York and Paris are all famous for their fashionable clothes shops. In recent years, some cities have developed huge shopping malls, though many of these are now situated in the suburbs rather than the inner city. One of the largest is in Edmonton, Canada, where the West Edmonton Mall boasts more than 800 stores, as well as restaurants, cinemas and a hotel.

Markets and bazaars

In the past, most villages and towns had a marketplace. These became even bigger and more important in growing cities. Today, they still exist in many cities, allowing traders to display their goods to both locals and visitors. In North Africa and south-west Asia these markets, known as bazaars or souks, are exciting places and are popular with tourists. Some are very old: the Khan al-Khalili bazaar, in Cairo, Egypt, grew

up around an inn that dates from 1390; Covent Garden, in London, began as a fruit and vegetable market in 1656. Both are still successful today.

Department stores

During the 19th century, large stores began selling a wide range of goods in separate departments, such as clothing, tools and food. The world's first was Le Bon Marché (meaning 'good buy' or 'bargain'), in Paris, which developed from a small shop into a large department store in the 1850s. By 1872, the East Side Bazaar had opened in New York, and

In many cities, such as here in Denver, Colorado, pedestrian zones have made shopping safer and more pleasant. This has also reduced pollution.

this developed into a store – Bloomingdale's – that by the 1920s covered a whole city block. In recent years, such famous stores have begun attracting shoppers from all over the world, bringing wealth and employment to their cities.

▲ *Part of the covered bazaar in Istanbul, the largest city in Turkey. This enormous bazaar is made up of 66 streets and has more than 4,000 shops, as well as a bank, a post office, and a place for worship.*

◄

Henry Charles Harrod took over a small grocer's shop in London in 1849. His shop developed into the famous department store called Harrods, which today has a staff of thousands.

Entertainment

In a city there is always something to do, and that is one of the great advantages of living there. This is also why a lot of people from the country or smaller towns like visiting cities. They have the choice of a wide range of sporting events, theatres and concerts. Every city has at least one large sports stadium, but city-dwellers also need their own open spaces where they can play games, run and walk, or simply relax. This need is met by a city's parks, which provide people with their own little bit of countryside. Even the biggest cities make room for large green areas. New York has Central Park, which is 4 kilometres long, and almost a kilometre wide,

▲ *Londoners have many parks to enjoy, including Hyde Park. This was originally a royal hunting park, but it was opened to the public in the early 17th century.*

and includes a lake and woods. In Tokyo, Ueno Park has museums, a zoo and a concert hall. This beautiful park is also famous for its spring displays of cherry tree blossoms.

On the stage

Playwrights, actors and almost everyone else involved in the theatre usually make their way to cities, because this is where most of the world's major theatres are. At London's Globe Theatre, it is now possible to watch a Shakespeare play in

Peking opera is a special kind of traditional Chinese drama that you can still see in Beijing. The plays are based on Chinese folk tales, and the actors wear elaborate costumes and make-up. ▶

the same way as Londoners did 400 years ago. This wooden theatre was rebuilt on the spot where the original burned down in the 17th century. Like London, New York has its own theatre district, located on the long street called Broadway. Nearby small theatres are known as off-Broadway, and experimental plays are put on in fringe theatres known as off-off-Broadway. Altogether, there are hundreds of theatres in New York.

Museums and galleries

Museums and art galleries are very important to scholars and students. In some cities, they can be visited for little or no charge. Some of the world's art galleries are so famous that people travel to cities simply to visit them. Some good European examples are the Louvre, in Paris, France; the Prado, in Madrid, Spain; the Hermitage, in St. Petersburg, Russia (which used to be the Winter Palace of the Russian tsars); and the Guggenheim Museum, in Bilbao, Spain, which opened in 1997.

The name of the Uffizi Gallery in Florence, Italy, stands for 'offices'. This is because the building was originally designed for government offices, but it soon became an art gallery. Florence has some of the finest galleries in the world.

◀

Attracting Visitors

Some cities attract millions of visitors each year because of their historical or religious significance. Every year around two million Muslims make a pilgrimage to Mecca, the holy city of Islam in Saudi Arabia. Up to half of them come from other countries on a special pilgrimage, called hajj. Varanasi, in northern India, annually attracts about one million Hindus, who go there to bathe in the holy waters of the Ganges River. In the same way, millions of Roman Catholics visit the Vatican, in Rome and hope to see the Pope, the spiritual head of their church. In many other historic cities, visitors come as tourists and holidaymakers. They stay in hotels, and go on sightseeing tours around the city.

▲ *Rodeos and other events have been held at the annual 10-day Calgary Stampede since 1923. About one million people go to Calgary, in Canada, for the festival.*

Venetian festivals

The unique city of Venice, in northern Italy, is built on islands linked by **canals**. It is popular with visitors from all over the world and has become a tourist attraction in itself. The locals have adapted to this, and many are involved in the tourist industry. The city has also attracted many international events, including festivals of

The ancient Venice carnival was revived in the 1980s. Revellers wear fantastic costumes and masks.

art, film, music and drama. The famous 10-day Venice carnival is similar to Mardi Gras in New Orleans, Louisiana, and every September there is a **regatta** on the Grand Canal, in which historic gondolas take to the water.

Growing tourist cities

Some new, growing cities would scarcely exist if it were not for tourism. Examples are the U.S. cities of Las Vegas, in Nevada, and Orlando, in Florida. Las Vegas had a population of just 64,000 in 1960. Forty years later, this had risen to nearly 300,000. The city is full of hotels and nightclubs, and about 30 million visitors go to the desert city every year. In Orlando, the main attractions are the theme parks of the Walt Disney World Resort, which opened in 1971. The parks are the main employers in the area.

Young visitors love Walt Disney World. This huge development led to many hotels, apartment buildings, restaurants, and shopping malls opening around Orlando.

Looking After Our Cities

Air pollution is a big problem for cities all over the world. The problem began a long time ago, when it was mainly caused by smoke and gases from factory chimneys. Many cities brought in regulations to control this, but now there is another cause for concern – car exhaust fumes. These fumes combine with the dust and dirt of the city to make an unhealthy **smog**. The inhabitants of megacities such as Los Angeles and Mexico City have suffered badly, and they and others have tried to reduce people's use of cars. In Mexico City and Athens, cars are allowed into the city only on certain days, according to their registration letter or number.

In London, a congestion charge was introduced in 2003. Drivers have to pay to go into the inner city, which helps reduce their numbers.

New communities

Cities are full of different neighbourhoods, and people from the same background often form their own community. During the 20th century, wealthier people tended to move away from city centres and settle in the outer city or suburbs. Many poorer people were not able to do this and stayed in the inner city. This has meant that many of the inner cities have poor housing and are in need of regeneration. At the same time, some districts that have been improved have created closed communities, behind gates and fences. People may feel this reduces crime, but it also separates communities. This is a problem to be faced in 21st century cities.

Into the future

The government of Brazil planned and built a new capital in 1960. Today, Brasilia has a population of 1.8 million. Other countries have tried making new towns, but they tend to get swallowed up by spreading cities nearby. In the future, the existing cities will surely get bigger. In many cases, separate suburbs will spread out until they meet each other. Then they will form a huge **megalopolis**. This is already happening in Japan, the United States, and parts of Europe.

▲ *A wealthy gated community in Dana Point, California.*

Part of modern Philadelphia, which is one of the oldest cities in the U.S. Today it lies in the middle of a growing megalopolis, with New York and Boston to the north and Baltimore and Washington, DC, to the south. ▲

Glossary

architects People who design buildings.

boulevards Wide streets lined with trees.

canals Artificial waterways.

cargo Goods carried by river, sea, road or air.

causeways Raised paths over water or wet land.

city-state An independent state made up of a city and its surrounding territory.

colony An area that is ruled by another country.

community All the people living in a particular place, especially those with shared interests.

commuter A person who travels regularly from the suburbs to the city.

exhaust fumes Waste gases pumped out from car engines.

Industrial Revolution The rapid development of machinery, factories and industry that began in the late 18th century.

inhabitants People who live in a particular place.

malnutrition Illness caused by lack of proper food.

megalopolis An area where large cities meet each other to make a 'supercity'.

monorail A passenger railway with a single track.

pedestrians People on foot; walkers.

populous With a large population.

port A place by a river or by the sea where boats can dock, load and unload.

poverty The state of not having enough money for basic necessities such as food and clothing.

regatta A series of boat races.

rural Relating to the countryside (as opposed to a town or city).

semi-detached houses Houses joined to another house on one side.

settlement A small village where people live permanently.

shanty A small, crudely built shack.

skyscrapers Very tall buildings with many stories.

slum An overcrowded, run-down district inhabited by poor people.

smog A mixture of smoke, fog and exhaust fumes.

suburbs Outer districts at the edge of a city.

terraced houses Rows of houses with no space in between.

urban Relating to a town or city (as opposed to the countryside).

Index